For Hans and Opa, who taught me to see.
—A.S.

For Darlene Robbins, my first and favorite poet.
—S.A.

His children look to heaven...
Open hands await His grace.
Blessed are the pure in heart,
for they shall see God's face.

Matthew 5:8

HIS CHILDREN

Published by Vantage Point Press, Saratoga, California

© 2003 Vantage Point Press, Inc.
Photos © Anita Schiller
Poems © 2002 Susan Noyes Anderson,
except "Peter" © 2002 Anita Schiller

Library of Congress Control Number: 2002096873

ISBN 0-9721661-1-4

Design: Toki Design, San Francisco

Printed in China

www.vantagepointpress.com

HIS CHILDREN

ANITA SCHILLER

POEMS BY SUSAN NOYES ANDERSON

VANTAGE POINT
PRESS

"...trailing clouds of glory do we come from God, who is our home." —William Wordsworth

INTRODUCTION

Who are we? From where did we come? What is our purpose in living? Answers to these questions can be found in a simple but life-altering awareness: we are all connected in the family of man, and that connection can be traced to a divine origin.

His Children explores this concept of divine origin and connectedness in photographs and poetry. We invite you, the reader, to join us as we experience a kaleidoscope of humanity through the various stages of life: from the innocent awakening of a newborn to the unbridled enthusiasm of a young child; from the questioning years of adolescence to the sensibility of adulthood and the comfortable confidence of maturity. Fear and faith, trial and triumph, heartache and happiness...all are represented in what is at once a celebration and a meditation on life and living. Candid photos, taken over a period of thirty years, are complemented by original poetry written in response to each image...the words a soundtrack adding layers of emotion to every page. Occasionally, we stop to marvel at the scenery as well.

The road we have traveled in creating this book has heightened our belief that we are children of a loving and benevolent God regardless of age, ethnicity, nationality or economic circumstance. This conviction has magnified our spirits, strengthened the love we have for every brother and sister, and reinforced our desire to understand each one of them. As you traverse these pages, meeting a few of His Children along the way, may you be touched by their greatness and reminded of your own.

Life is an adventure, and we? The adventurers.

Anita Schiller   Susan Noyes Anderson

"For all the stars, like burning dew, are luminous and luring footprints of souls adventurous as you." —Sara Teasdale

Step by step, we come to thee;
Thy light is a beacon for all to see.

Thy word is a lamp unto my feet, and a light unto my path.

Psalms 119:105

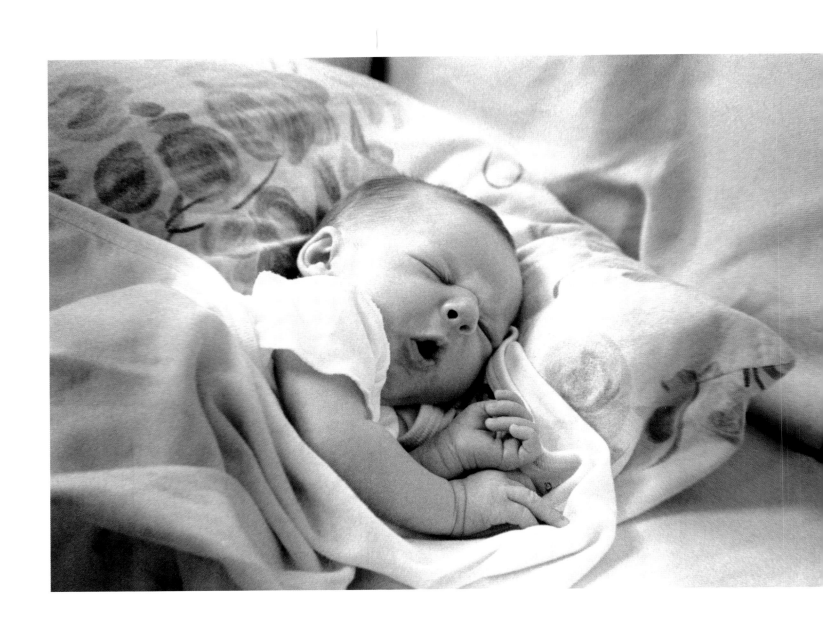

Welcome, baby, to the world!
I wonder who you'll be?
You are a miracle—God's own,
a child of destiny.

GAVIN
SARATOGA, CALIFORNIA, 2000

Beginnings speak of innocence
and confidence and trust.
Believing is indigenous;
the world is safe and just
until life proves it otherwise.
In lonely, aching need,
when faith and hope are tenuous,
...a little child shall lead.

Isaiah 11:6

NICHOLAS
SARATOGA, CALIFORNIA, 2000

A little girl
A laugh, a sigh
A sparkle in
A soft, blue eye

A little shy
A little bold
A secret kept
A story told

A hand to hold
A lock to curl
A daisy chain
A skip, a twirl

A little girl
A woman's start
A work of grace
A work of art

CLAIRE
FOLSOM, CALIFORNIA, 2002

A child is playing in the sand.
   What secrets does he understand?
He knows the magic of the sea;
   the evidence is in his hand.

A blond head turns away from me
   but I can feel the mystery.
It's in the line his body makes...
   the bend of elbow, neck and knee.

And watching him, my soul awakes.
   His beauty swells and crests and breaks
in child-like wonder on my heart.
   His innocence is all it takes.

Perhaps the ocean plays a part
in summoning this healer's art.
   The boy entranced me from the start.
   The boy entranced me from the start.

SAND PAINTING
FT. CRONKHITE, CALIFORNIA, 1968

My friend and I go all around;
    together we are always found.
Sometimes we run and shout and play;
    sometimes we sit upon the ground.

My friend and I could talk all day
    or just be quiet. Either way,
We always find enough to do;
    we always find enough to say.

My friend and I are tried and true...
    when skies are gray, when skies are blue.
We don't give up. We laugh. We cry.
    We love each other, through and through.

We're lucky ones, my friend and I.
We watch the golden hours fly;
    and earn what only time can buy,
    and earn what only time can buy.

UNTITLED
CENTRAL PARK, NY, 1966

Alone is hard to be
Deprived of company
No one comes in or out
Nobody moves about
And nothing to begin
The barriers close in
Deprived of company
Alone is hard to be

Our children stand witness;
their natures record
nothing less, nothing more
than they see.
Then what shall we show them?
The pure or the dross?
Will the world we create
foil or free?

CURB YOUR DOG
NEW YORK, 1966

Too many sorrows I have known,
　　too many sadnesses unsaid.
A lake of woe surrounds my heart,
　　the last remains of tears unshed.

DISCARDED
CUZCO, PERU, 1999

The water is wide and shimmers clear.
    Each tree's reflection, straight and tall,
stands witness to the majesty
    of God, who has created all.

In quiet places He draws near;
    let any who would seek release
withdraw into the wilderness
    and find in Him a sense of peace.

SOLITUDE
LEXINGTON RESERVOIR, LOS GATOS,
CALIFORNIA, 1998

SIMPLE PLEASURES
AGUAS CALIENTES, PERU, 1999

Though some have more and some have less
All have the gifts that He imparts
His children will find happiness

Not in belongings they possess
But in the longings of their hearts
Though some have more and some have less

The measure of a soul's success
Lies in the sacred, inner parts
His children will find happiness

In days of bliss or deep distress
Each child can learn the Master's arts
Though some have more and some have less

All have the power to heal and bless
All feel the hope of fresh new starts
His children will find happiness

In every feeling they express
In joy and all its counterparts
Though some have more and some have less
His children will find happiness

God's little ones are most content.
    They make no arrogant demand,
but try to fill each simple need
    by taking on the task at hand.

SMALL FRY
CUZCO, PERU, 1999

Baby dolls and buggies
    A stroll beside the lake
Curly heads and sunsuits
    What memories these make

A bandaid on an owie
    Two faded tennis shoes
More time than little hands can count
    And yet, no time to lose

head bowed
hand clenched
brow furrowed
body benched
feet tapping
shoulders hunched
mind in motion
paper scrunched
dawn to dusk
night 'til morn
one more time
a writer's born

THE WRITER
MILL VALLEY, CALIFORNIA, 1968

With brush in hand
the world unfolds
ain't color grand
each stroke explodes
in shades of
possibility
of life and art
and what can be

THE PAINTER
MILL VALLEY, CALIFORNIA, 1968

Beauty cannot enter where we do not leave a friendly space.
Poems began as empty pages, masterpieces as a trace.

Every note must stand alone before it makes a lullabye.
Every tree has greater stature viewed against a naked sky.

Life is simple; letting go creates a place for hopes and dreams.
Barren walls and open floors make room for ever-changing themes.

CHAIR, DRESSER, MIRROR
TUSCANY, ITALY, 1998

We all step through the looking glass,
   but each one takes a different ride.
Some fall head-first like Alice did,
   while others choose a measured stride.

Who trusts enough to nibble life
   will grow or shrink accordingly.
Who waits and watches from afar
   will likely find herself at sea.

Beware the Jabberwock, indeed,
   but neither yield nor disappear.
Just glance back through the looking glass
   and wave and whisper, "I'm still here."

THE WAVE
CENTRAL PARK, NEW YORK, 1966

Twas brillig, and the scayful tods
   did clump and scramlick on the Lew.
All mazy were the giboren...
   (Do you love Lewis Carroll too?)

CHILD'S PLAY
CENTRAL PARK, NEW YORK, 1966

When do men lose the urge to climb
and run to ground?
Where children see a peak sublime
the grown-ups look at rock and grime,
then shake their heads and turn around,
exchanging dreams for feet of clay.
Who gives up heights becomes earthbound.
Youth slips away
without a sound.

there's wisdom here
the power of three
the power of surf
and sand and sea
the power to kneel
upon the ground
the power to build
on something sound
the power to feel
that nothing ends
the power of three
the power of friends
the power of surf
and sand and sea
there's wisdom here
the power of three

BEACH DAY
FT. CRONKHITE, CALIFORINA, 1968

*L*ord how manifold are thy works;
   we all have eyes to see.
The earth is full of thy riches;
   our hearts sing praise to thee.

Thou touchest the hills and they smoke;
   in thy light, shadows flee.
Our meditations shall be sweet;
   our joyful spirits, free.

Psalms 104:24, 32, 34

TUSCAN MORNING
TUSCANY, ITALY, 1998

Come on in.
The water's fine
        and frigid too.
No matter.
He who presses
        forward
shall be blessed
        with teeth
        that chatter.

Walk down the lane where childhood ends
　　and stop at the old oak tree—
the sturdy one whose branches reach
　　as high as high can be.

Circle around and look once more
　　on amber days gone by.
Settle your roots in solid earth
　　and gather strength to fly.

FARANA
LOS GATOS, CALIFORNIA, 2001

Somewhere behind the angle of his face
    resides the carefree child he used to be.
The soft curves yield to time, and in their place
    emerge the strong lines of maturity.

A man is in the making; guard him well.
    Let love and justice teach what hate abhors.
Respect his right to prove he can excel,
    and he will view the world through open doors.

NUBIAN PRINCE
MILL VALLEY, CALIFORNIA, 1969

Don't mess with me
Don't crowd my space
You're in my way
You're in my face
I won't be you
I can't be me
I'm moving out
I'm breaking free
Have some respect
This is no stage
You're not in charge
I'm legal age
Don't preach at me
I'll just say no
My life is calling
Gotta go

CATHYE
SAUSALITO, CALIFORNIA, 1969

Our feet propel us swiftly through
   this earthly promenade.
These words suspend the race: *Be still,*
   and know that I am God.

The steps we take in haste feel free,
   yet leave behind a shallow print.
To walk with God is everything
   but we do love a sprint!

Psalms 46:10

The world is flying by, and we?
　　As fast as wind, as free as air.
Our destination? We don't know.
　　We're much too busy getting there!

ON THE MOVE
FLORENCE, ITALY, 1998

The past stands patiently behind our backs
    Invisible at times, or just unseen
Obscured by haste and waste and quantum facts
    Upstaged by beeper, phone and fax machine

Upstaged by beeper, phone and fax machine
    Today's communication leaves no tracks
We hold hands with a plastic go-between
    The past stands patiently behind our backs

CELLULAR TRIO
FLORENCE, ITALY, 1998

If ever earth and sky should spin away
    and love and truth lie crumbled at your feet,
when all around and in you cries defeat
    and hope and faith seem merely words to say—

Say nothing; hear Him whisper to your soul:
"My peace lies in acceptance, not control."

And the peace of God, which passeth all understanding,
shall keep your hearts and minds through Christ Jesus.

Philippians 4:7

SPINNING
LOS GATOS, CALIFORNIA, 1998

to see her hands
their beauty weave
restored my faith
made my heart conceive
of a graceful life
and a peaceful day
a man and wife
a place to stay

THE WEAVER
SAUSALITO, CALIFORNIA, 1969

The world shows many faces;
    every life holds sundry charms.
But universal is our yearning
    for a mother's arms.

MOTHER AND CHILD
PISAC RUINS, URUBAMBA RIVER VALLEY
PERU, 1999

It's found in the tilt of a curly head,
the line of a jaw or chin.
The family tie is ageless, eternal,
and welcomes the stranger in.

UNTITLED
MONTALCINO, ITALY, 1998

A kinder soul I've seldom known
than the one I call Brother—
yes, even my own.

He's honest and true and filled with grace.
The depth of his goodness
is etched in his face.

The middle child, selfless peacemaker.
He's often the giver
and rarely the taker.

A greater friend I've seldom known
than the one I call Brother—
yes, even my own.

—*Anita Schiller*

I do believe that long ago in the eternities,

  I was a bosom friend to you and you a friend to me.

We shared a bond, an understanding that was quick and sure.

  I wonder if we knew that it would deepen and endure.

The tie between us had to be the everlasting kind,

  for even in this earthly life our paths have intertwined.

We were sisters, bound by a love so meaningful and rare,

  that we must have had an inkling of the destiny we'd share.

And once prepared to leave the Father we had always known,

  surely we joined hands and vowed to help each other home.

Now that we find ourselves mother and daughter on this earth,

  please don't forget the vow we made and its inherent worth.

For though I know that in this life the burden rests with me,

  the promise those two sisters made was for eternity.

THE KISS
SAUSALITO, CALIFORNIA, 1997

How does the child whose gift is hope,
   whose eager hands and shining eyes
   embrace the possibilities
   and seek the prize
Become the child whose gift is lost
   between the shadows and the years,
   whose empty heart is framed in eyes
   devoid of tears?
And who will hold the hands that reach?
And who will lift the heads that bow?
   The answer lies within us all.
   The time is now.

DESPAIR
AGUAS CALIENTES, PERU, 1999

Who am I? A mystery—
  my thoughts unknown, my world unseen.
How much of life and light is lost
  behind a self-made screen?

UNTITLED
TUSCANY, ITALY, 1998

The lens of mystery may shield
a soul laid bare.
Sometimes injustice must be healed
before the layers are revealed,
and only then to those who care
enough to listen and to heed.
Respect, though sadly all too rare,
is each man's need
and just, and fair.

SHADES
SAUSALITO, CALIFORNIA, 1969

Each child of God wears dignity,
    a heritage he brings to earth.
No ragged coat, however soiled,
    diminishes intrinsic worth.

The humble understand this truth;
    the proud look down and put on greed.
They care not for the hungry soul;
    they cannot fill the aching need.

Be wary of the hollow ones,
    the empty people walking free.
In choosing not to give love,
    they surrender their humanity.

FASHION STATEMENT
FLORENCE, ITALY, 1998

The world keeps churning, turning round
It does not stop for those who fall
The lost ones sleep upon the ground

Unloved, unnoticed and unfound
They pay no heed to clarion call
The world keeps churning, turning round

As tinkling tongues of brass expound
On ways and means to honor all
The lost ones sleep upon the ground

They cannot hear the cymbal's sound
Nor do they fit the protocol
The world keeps churning, turning round

While sages speak in tones profound
Their words step over those who crawl
The lost ones sleep upon the ground

They dream no more; their hearts are bound
And no one comes to breach the wall
The world keeps churning, turning round
The lost ones sleep upon the ground

Though I speak with the tongues of men and of angels,
and have not charity, I am become as sounding brass,
or a tinkling cymbal.

1 Corinthians 13:1

THE SLEEPER
NEW YORK, 1966

Behold, He stands at the door and knocks,
   Will any let this Servant in?
For He who drank the bitter cup
   would sup with those He raised from sin.

Knock and the door shall be opened.
   His promise lives for all mankind.
Ask and it shall be given you...
   Seek, and surely ye shall find.

We have His words: *I am the door...*
   By me...if any enter in,
he shall be saved...I am the way.
   May truth and life be ours through Him.

Matthew 7:7
John 10:9, 12:47, 14:6

THE DOOR
TUSCANY, ITALY, 1998

Sit down with me, and let us seek
    a respite from the cold and bleak.
Lay down the bundles that you hold,
    and listen to the words I speak.

No longer young, must we be old?
    Have we no stories left untold?
Are there no dreams for us to dream?
    Can we be neither brave, nor bold?

Men are not always as they seem;
    they turn from ice to slush to steam.
Show me the sun that cannot rise,
    the soul too wretched to redeem.

Show me the kindness in your eyes,
    the love that sees beyond disguise.
Help me believe the sun will rise;
    there is no truth in empty skies.

UNTITLED
URUBAMBA RIVER VALLEY, PERU, 1999

Her eyes look past the window pane,
  beyond the shutters and the years.
She hears the laughing children, sees
  but does not see them through her tears.

A ray of sunlight warms her cheek;
  her lips know well the taste of rain.
The window of her spirit opens
  wide upon this daughter's pain.

At times, we look out on the world
and gain a clearer view,
but often we must fall to earth
to witness what is true.

THE VIEW
TUSCANY, ITALY, 1998

We make of Life an enemy or friend,
    depending on our hospitality...
our choice to welcome Her or let Her be,
    our right to denigrate or to defend.

Her face is ever changing as the moon,
    yet She is fixed and forthright as the stars.
Her gifts are wisdom, joy and battle scars;
    and all must dance, unbidden, to Her tune.

Life comes to us unbridled; shall we hide?
    Or will we, through the pleasure and the pain,
embrace the greatest heights we can attain
    and smile upon the world with hearts flung wide?

UNTITLED
BUONCONVENTO, ITALY, 1998

A merry heart will not be bound
  by winter snow or frozen earth.
No weathered brow or soil-stained cheek
  can quell the buoyant lines of mirth.

A merry heart is medicine;
  it worketh good for all mankind.
Instinctively, we reach for joy:
  Children of Light, and unresigned.

LAUGHING WOMAN
URUBAMBA RIVER VALLEY, PERU, 1999

The open heart is never quite alone,
    neither in empty room nor silent street;
and though there may be none to hold or greet,
    for those who've loved, these joys are not unknown.
Look forward, when it seems that life has flown,
    or tarry where the memories are sweet.
Let hope and wisdom dominate defeat,
    and solitude find value all her own.
The lonely hide behind their shuttered eyes
    and, clutching isolation to their chests,
leave freer souls to sit beneath blue skies
    and feel the warmth of friendship in their breasts.
One locks the door, pulls down the shade and sighs.
The other opens to a bright sunrise.

TATTING
MONTALCINO, ITALY, 1998

TATTING
MONTALCINO, ITALY, 1998

The peaceful tinkle of a bell,
a sunrise dawning clear;
The Shepherd may not be in view,
but He is always near.

THE FLOCK
TUSCANY, ITALY, 1998

Come, speak to me of times gone by.
 Remind me of our carefree youth.
Recall with me those nights we sang
 and laughed and thought we knew the truth.

Come, speak to me of times gone by.
 Remind me of my dancing feet.
Recall with me those days we knew
 the world was ours, and life was sweet.

REFLECTIONS ON ANOTHER DAY
BUONCONVENTO, ITALY, 1998

Oh, for a son
when my head is bowed,
and years have lined my face—
A stalwart son
with a gentle heart,
where I still hold
a mother's place.

Oh, for a son
when eyes grow dim
and memories recede—
A spirited son,
a steadfast son,
who sees but does not
fear my need.

MARKET DAY
MONTALCINO, ITALY, 1998

Thrust in the sickle;
the land is rich, and
the fruit thereof is sweet.
The labor of love
has been performed;
the cycle is complete.

Thrust in the sickle,
though youth has gone
and strength is on the wane.
The vineyard calls; its
master knows the joy
that hides in pain.

The old regard the new
with disapproving view,
resentful of the day
ebullience slips away.
A dreadful thing, it seems
to let go of one's dreams.
A pity too, for age
is just a stage.

DISAPPROVAL
SAUSALITO, CALIFORNIA, 1969

All living things must yield;
the cycle is revealed.
A leaf, once green, turns brown
then, falling to the ground,
dissolves to fertilize
a seedling on the rise.
As rain becomes the dew,
so every end is new.

FALL LEAVES
LOS GATOS, CALIFORNIA, 1998

Wanted, one beautiful day at the shore;
a good log for sitting; an ocean to roar;
a paper for reading; a bit of a breeze;
a pair of bare feet (hold the sand, if you please);
some driftwood, some shells, and the smell of the sea.
Now cut me a deal. Did I hear you say "FREE"?!

BAREFOOTIN'
FT. CRONKHITE, CALIFORNIA, 1968

Life has its simple pleasures:
   the shade of a sturdy tree,
a cooling sip of water,
   an old friend's company.

SHADY RESPITE
TUSCANY, ITALY, 1998

In life, there is a symmetry,
   a balance that bespeaks a plan,
and he who treads a humble path
   will find in him a peaceful man.

Look up; the leaves adorn the trees,
   then fall to earth beneath your feet.
Look down; each stone could grace a pillar
   or be crushed into concrete.

True harmony is always found
   within the singing of a song.
The road will show you where it leads,
   and if the way is short or long.

PERSPECTIVE
MONTALCINO, ITALY, 1998

In the end, every lonely and narrow trail
    has its weathered and well-worn gate;
and a traveler's steps, whether firm or frail,
    move him surely toward his fate.

Judge not by the faded, discolored wood;
    look with eyes that are stripped of pride.
The joys of entry are lost or found
    in what lies on the other side.

THE GATE
TUSCANY, ITALY, 1998

Times Square with all its cheer
cannot revive a year.
And no amount of pique
will slow a passing week.
No force on earth can stay
the closing of a day.
So give in...Count some sheep.
The dawn will keep.

CLOSED
SAUSALITO, CALIFORNIA, 1969

REWIND
A Slightly Different Look at *His Children*

There is something about photographers that allows—no, forces—them to see the extraordinary in everyday occurrences, to glimpse beauty where others find only pain or suffering, to relish those small and seemingly insignificant details which escape the uninitiated eye.

In my family, we joke that photography is a genetic disorder. My grandfather learned the craft in Germany and worked as a photographer and teacher of photography to sustain himself when he immigrated to Palestine in the early 1930s. For my father, a gifted architect, photography was as natural and integral a part of his work as drawing and design. With his office downstairs in our home, I spent hours as a young girl sitting on a stool in the darkroom watching him work. He gave me my first camera when I was eight or nine years old; I developed my first roll of film at age ten. By the time I took my first "real" photography class in high school, the seeds of our family genetic disorder, firmly planted in my soul, had blossomed into full-blown obsession. I photographed everything and everyone: rocks, flowers, sunrises, sunsets, friends, strangers—who or whatever passed before my lens. I even stood vigil at the mailbox, waiting for the latest *National Geographic* or *Life Magazine* to arrive and inspire me. By age 19, I had begun to formulate ideas for a photographic book. The ideas would remain with me for years...waiting for their day to come.

In the meantime, my interest in watching people grew. A camera in hand made it easy, even acceptable, to scrutinize every face in minute detail without seeming to stare, observing personalities, similarities and differences closely. Over the years, traveling to faraway places and experiencing the ups and downs of life helped me understand my fascination with photography a little better. I will always have that drive to "capture the moment," but equally strong is the need to express my love for humanity by sharing the inherent beauty, complex nature, unique gifts and defining attributes of each individual—things that can only be seen when one takes the time to stop and look.

Thank you for taking this journey with me—for taking the time to stop and look. I feel certain that those of His Children who grace these pages have already touched your lives in uniquely personal ways, but may I invite you to visit them again? This time, you will have the opportunity to watch over my shoulder and see exactly as I saw—through the viewfinder of the camera. With your permission, let's rewind and look once more, with a slightly different eye. —*A.S.*

THROUGH THE EYES OF A CHILD

My parents allowed me to spend the summer of 1966 with a couple of elderly aunts in Manhattan. This initial visit to NY was also my first experience away from home. At 13 years old, I was simultaneously intrigued and disturbed by the things I saw.

Because my aunts lived nearby, I visited Central Park often. Caught up in their innocence and excitement, I enjoyed photographing the children at play there. Am I wrong, or does Lewis Carroll look a bit weary from all the climbing, laughing, scampering children?

The Caucasian children played, happily unaware of anyone around them, while the one black child stopped to wave. The man was lost in his paper, while the woman sat watching. Was there something in this scene about insiders and outsiders, those who trust and those who watch?

In contrast to other photos from this series, this first one left me with a sense of filth and poverty—the pieces of paper on the ground, the children sitting in the dirt, their bare feet, the empty benches and the fence rails. In both of these, the absence of an adult nearby disturbed me. It seemed an odd place for young children to play alone.

I had never seen anyone sleeping on the street before. Previously, my only glimpse of homelessness or drunkenness had been on the occasional shopping trip to San Francisco with my mother. I remember feeling scared walking down Market Street and seeing the "bums" on the street. Understanding that people really lived like this was a humbling revelation.

I remember thinking about the odd juxtaposition of the girl and the sign above her. "Keep New York Clean" it says, but look at the trash on the ground at the base of the pole. "Curb your dog." Did people think this little girl was a dog because of her skin color? Was she wrongly considered trash and unclean? In retrospect, these seem like deep things for a 13 year-old to be thinking about.

During the summer between my sophomore and junior years in high school I worked as a teacher's assistant in a Headstart program. I photographed some of the children in class and on outings to the beach.

These girls were growing up in one of the most affluent counties in the US, yet they lived in a ghetto within that county—an almost exclusively black community with only one road in and one road out. Their small, densely populated neighborhood was plagued with alcohol and drug abuse, broken families, neglect and poverty. Although only 10 miles away, a trip to the beach was a rare treat, one these girls seemed to enjoy thoroughly.

This photo begs a question or two. What is he doing? What does he look like? Is he happy or sad? There is mystery in not seeing his face. The gentle curves of his hair, the stripes of his clothes and the faint pattern where he has smoothed the sand in front of him suggest some grand design. I like his little hands and the hint of his sandy bare feet.

Peace and quiet. A sunny day. Warm enough to take off one's shoes and socks (neatly lined up on the log, of course), but not so warm to take off one's jacket or hat. Does the newspaper under his feet tell us "I like the beach, but not enough to take it home with me?"

Whether it's a statue of Lewis Carroll or a tree, put a child near an object that can be climbed, and it will be...And the more who can climb at the same time, the better. What's behind this urge to rise and conquer? Is it a child's curious nature? Is it an early manifestation of our constant desire to reach greater heights? Is it the fearlessness and innocence of childhood?

Imbued with innocence, children have few inhibitions. It is a wonderful thing to watch when a child's creative talents are unleashed. This little girl was thoroughly immersed in her art. I can still feel her energy and exuberance. There's no stopping her.

The objective of the Headstart program was to provide early childhood development programs and services to economically disadvantaged children, preparing them for successful entry into the public education system. This boy was a classic example of a child with the desire and capacity to learn, but perhaps little or no support at home. He would stay in the classroom and work on his writing when the other children went out to play. The photo embodies his hard work and determination, even when all the desks and chairs around him are empty. And what of the crumpled papers beside him—signs of impatience, frustration, a striving for perfection, his failed attempts?

INNOCENCE LOST

The late 60s, my high school years, were challenging. It was a time of growing up too fast. The war in Vietnam was raging, civil rights loomed large in people's minds, the Black Panther party and black pride were the news of the day and the youth of America, myself included, were struggling to know who we were. These photos of youth during that time exemplify the inner struggles that were and are a part of growing up.

A proud face hides behind shades meant to keep the world (reflected in the lenses) from getting in, to keep outsiders from getting too close. Standing at his side, however, the black almond-shaped eye... window to his soul...is clearly visible. We see strength and vulnerability, pride and uncertainty, a statement and a question.

This portrait of a high school friend has long been a favorite of mine. The way one side of her face and the background fall in total shadow is compelling, and the light on her working hands draws you into the heart of the photo. I see mystery in the wisp of hair in her face, the length of it over her opposite shoulder, the texture of the weaving, the lace tablecloth and lightly blowing curtain on her side. The sense of calm belies the reality of that time.

The carefree young man in the foreground and his girlfriend were laughing and kidding around, oblivious to the disapproving looks coming from the older man in the background. Had he forgotten the more rambunctious days of his own youth, or did he remember and begrudge their fun because his time had passed?

AWAKENINGS

My father passed away in July 1998, at the age of 81. I had seen him the day before, and though we didn't speak of it, he knew he was dying. His mood was light-hearted as I drove him to a doctor's appointment. We laughed and joked as always. I noticed he seemed very much at peace with himself and the world, the mark of a man with no unfinished business. I spoke with him about a trip I was taking in a few days to the Tuscan region of Italy. When we returned to the house, he had me pull out some old photos he had taken while stationed in Sienna during WWII. He reminisced about the experience while we looked through the beautiful old B&W photos, telling me how much he loved Sienna and the surrounding area. I was touched. A very private man, he had never shared that experience with me before. We parted with hugs, smiles and "I love you." He went to bed that night as usual. He awoke around 4:00 a.m., got out of bed and went to the refrigerator, fixed a bowl of his favorite vanilla ice cream, then returned to bed. He died in his sleep, perhaps dreaming of idyllic days in Sienna. Ten days later, at the urging of my family, I was on my way to Italy with the tender memory of my father and his recollections fresh in my mind.

I tried to photograph the things my father would have photographed, mostly the beautiful architecture and landscape of the region. But everywhere I went, I was more captivated by Tuscan life than its inanimate objects; and so, as is my wont to do, those are the impressions I gathered.

I felt a certain irony in this view of three young people standing by the cathedral in Florence, Italy's Piazza del Duomo, yet this is a typical scene in a bustling tourist city—one, for that matter, which could take place in any large city in the world. Here is the perfect juxtaposition of patience and haste—the cathedral, the

oldest in Florence, built during the 4th or 5th Century, A.D., and the people on their cell phones representing the speed of change as we know it today. The contrast of things spiritual and worldly is seen here also, often existing side by side and usually with vast distance between them. Another thing that struck me was the three individuals, themselves. Although they have all chosen the same place to stand, there is no indication that there is any relationship between them. They might be best friends or they might be total strangers. They are all in the act of communicating (presumably), but none with each other. They appear to be connected only by space, time and the fact that they are all youthful; each has a bag; each uses the left hand to hold the phone; none are smiling. Nothing more can be determined about them. Finally, I was attracted to the lines of the background. The cathedral walls are solid and stable, but the lines are somewhat chaotic, with some vertical and some horizontal. Again, it made me think of the stability and security of things spiritual, and the chaotic nature of life in the world.

In both of these photos, the hurried pace of the big city is apparent. The Vespa is the vehicle of choice for getting around the narrow crowded streets quickly and easily. They are everywhere. I was experimenting that day with capturing motion, so I stood on a corner for about 10 minutes and photographed every passing scooter, panning the camera as it went by. Of all the resulting photos, this was my favorite, largely because of the driver—no pun intended. The photo of the people walking across the piazza was taken the same day. The moving bodies had a ghost-like appearance—now you see them, now you don't. It reminded me that life is like that sometimes. We're in such a hurry to go places and do things that we don't linger long enough to even leave an impression.

Walking down a mostly deserted street, I saw this man with what were probably his only belongings contained in a couple of plastic grocery bags and spread out before him on the ground. The cruel irony of the scene caught my attention. Inside the window of a fashionable men's clothing store stand three mannequins who appear to be passing judgment on the poor homeless man. At first glance it is not apparent that they are mannequins. They are clearly on the inside, and he is clearly an outsider. They are the haves…They even have an extra pair of shoes, representing the excess of the world. He is the have-not. And yet, while they notice and judge him, he expresses a quiet defiance and self-confidence of his own. He has chosen to stand where he has, with no regard for them. The man is in front of their store, his back turned to them, doing his own thing, making his own fashion statement.

Maybe it's something to do with being an architect's daughter, but I often photograph doors and windows when I travel. In the end, the photos are almost always more interesting to me when they have people in them. How wonderful for me that the people in Italy seem to live in their windows and doorways. Sometimes they hang out the windows and participate in life in the streets below, and sometimes they merely act as observers. In this case, the woman in the window is barely noticeable as she blends in with the curvy reflections in the glass. There is a certain sadness in her face. Perhaps she is mourning the loss of a loved one. Perhaps she is reminiscing about better times. Perhaps she is lonely and wishing she had the courage to venture to the other side of the glass. The lines of the shutters and the bars of the porch railing seem to imprison her in a private world. And yet, the soft curve of the railing says that the prison is perhaps more imaginary than real. The texture of the wall gives a feeling of sadness and tiredness, mirrored again in her face.

Unlike the previous photo, this woman is not a prisoner in her home. She is smiling and as open as her window. She uses her window as a place of strength from which to connect with the outside world. She gazes directly into your eyes, wanting to know as much about you as you do about her. She uses the rail on her window as a support, not as a barrier or something behind which to hide.

Although this photo has a similar feel to the first of the window series, it is not at all what it appears. The feeling of the photo is "deeper" than its reality. The mystery of the person in the window (muted by the screen), the sense of isolation and loneliness, the texture of the wall (stone, old brick, dead and living vines), and the asymmetry of it all appeal to me. In reality, the young man in the window is neither lonely nor pondering the outside world in a serious way. He is listening to a mutual acquaintance of ours talking to him from the yard below and telling him about our dinner plans for the evening. While the wall and the composition give the appearance of a dreary gray day, it was in fact a warm sunny afternoon, with lots of laughter and friendship and happy thoughts to go around.

I visited Montalcino several times during my stay in Tuscany. It is a lovely small town perched high upon a hillside, overlooking the fertile farming region below. I loved walking up and down the narrow streets where the people were friendly and warm. As I passed this girl and young man I was struck by their good looks and charming smiles. I asked if I could take their photo, and they happily obliged. At the time I thought they were father and daughter, but others have suggested subsequently that perhaps they are brother and sister. It really doesn't matter. Their familial connection is apparent, even in their loosely entwined legs; their happiness contagious.

As with so many of my favorite photos, this one just happened to come into my field of vision when I was lucky enough to have my camera with me. I was in the car, waiting for a friend to finish using the pay phone, when I noticed this group of old men in my side-view mirror. I had seen them almost every time I passed that way and wondered what they did at the cafe each afternoon. I imagined they sat around and talked about days gone by. I loved the way that the mirror framed them. I loved that I could observe them with my camera without intruding.

On one of my excursions to Montalcino, I climbed up a steep side street solely for the purpose of photographing this elderly woman as she sat and tatted lace. In her doorway, she could maintain an active con-nection with her surrounding friends and neighbors. Though she sat in quiet solitude, something about her said she was not alone. She seemed to be entirely at peace with her-self and the world around her. I love the strong diagonal lines, the hint of light on the window frame, the rail and her hair, the rich texture of the street and the walls.

In a tiny open market in Montalcino, a mother and son worked together. I watched for awhile as she conducted her business, then asked the son if I might photograph her. He happily consented. I imagine a story of some sort for each and every line and wrinkle in her face. Her white hair shines like the pure wisdom of a life filled with experience. The connection between mother and son is tangible…They even wear the same watch. The contrast of

his radiant smile and her serious look is pleasing. The old-fashioned scale speaks of a time gone by, but still very real in their lives. The simplicity of life makes it rich.

These men were caretakers of the 200-year-old farm I visited for several days. I found them relaxing on a warm afternoon after lunch, living the unhurried life of a farming community. The stark simplicity of the scene sends one back in time a bit.

Rolling hills with vineyards are the essence of Tuscany. This elderly farmer tends to his grapes, one vine at a time, a life-long endeavor. He uses no big equipment or machinery, just a sickle and lots of love. Anyone who is still breathing is not too old to work.

Where there is symmetry, there is order. Where there is order, there is room for peace and contemplation. I see a gentle symmetry in the row of trees on the left and the row of stone pillars on the right…the leaves on the ground and the leaves on the branches above. The path gently slopes and rounds off at the top, leaving you to wonder where it leads. The elderly man at the wall adds to the sense of contemplation.

On an early morning jog through gentle hills, I heard bells ringing from afar. Rounding the corner, I saw a large flock of sheep. "Jingaling jingaling." Their bells floated on the breeze as they grazed in the field. The early morning light was soft pink and orange, and the sun-dried meadow was a beautiful gold. The sheep were rolling balls of cotton. It was only as I approached the fence at the edge of the pasture that I discovered their shepherd, the dog lying near the left side of the photo. As I got close, he charged the fence and moved the sheep away from this unwanted intrusion. As soon as he sensed any possible danger had passed, he settled back into his inconspicuous waiting and watching position. It made me think of how the Spirit gives us gentle little nudges when we are straying from the path or approaching danger.

I can't witness such a scene without thinking about God's incredible gift to His children—the creation of the earth. The early morning light gives the fog amazing billowy texture. It lights the hedge that runs diagonally down the hill as if it were shining only on that spot. I love the zig-zag texture created by the furrows of the field and a few scattered hay bales. It speaks of peace and serenity.

In this, the disposable age, we are accustomed to discarding things just because they are old. Somehow we seem to value things that are new and shiny more than those that are old and well-worn. The gate and door are rich with interesting lines, the contrasting textures of the wood, the brick, the metal hinge and latch, and even the little bits of grass. Perhaps they are like the face of an elderly person. The lines and texture reveal something about the kind of life they might have lived. What lies behind is a complete mystery to us, unless they decide to open up and let us in to see.

In my room on the farm, the walls were bare except for a small mirror. The floor was made of terra cotta tile. Despite the room's austerity, it was a warm, comfortable place to stay. The sounds of birds and crickets filled the air each morning. The smells of sun-drenched fields and dust filled my nostrils. A light wind blowing through wispy curtains cooled the afternoon. I like the soft shadows on the wall from the chair and dresser, and the absence of any reflection in the mirror. It was a place to sleep, not to stay. It invited you to go elsewhere and experience what was outside the room, not hibernate.

The window was like another invitation to journey outside the confines of my room. The contrast of the walls in deep shadow, the texture of the old window frame and the muted tile and tree branch all say "Go."

OTHER WORLDS, OTHER CHILDREN

My husband and I have visited many countries around the world. This series of photos was taken on a 1999 Peruvian trip to hike the Inca Trail and visit Machu Picchu. Life in the Andes is harsh. The air is thin at the extreme altitudes. The land is beautiful but rugged. The sun and the wind are intense. The people have little in the way of worldly goods.

There is a sense of incredible sadness and weariness about this beautiful little girl, who appears to carry the weight of the world on her shoulders. She, like the torn scraps of paper in her hand and the clothes she is wearing, seems to have been discarded by the world.

I noticed this little boy while we ate lunch and waited for our train from Aguas Calientes back to Cuzco. Aguas Calientes is the end of the line of the railroad that runs through the Urubamba River valley to Machu Picchu. For this little boy, a rock to play with and a dog for a friend seemed to be all that was needed for contentment. He practically turned himself upside down as he tried to get the sleeping dog's attention without getting too close. When that failed, he became engrossed in playing with a rock and scratching out his mark on the railroad track. He was in his own world, completely oblivious to anything else going on around him.

Wherever there are tourists, there are young Quechua girls with their babies, ready and willing to be photographed for a few pesos. I rarely pay someone to pose, but this girl appealed to me. It may have been her baby's black eyes and wide, pudgy feet. A young woman in her teens, her life is decidedly different from young women her age in my town. Her filthy hands are worn from working the land and braving the arid mountain air. The hat, the woven blanket (which allows her to easily carry her baby on her back), and the full skirt are typical of the dress for women in the region.

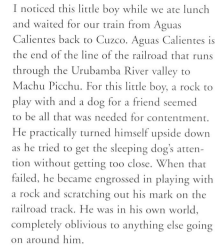

On the train to Cuzco, we stopped at a tiny village where passengers could buy drinks, fruit and other odds and ends. These two men were sitting by the side of the track. Most likely their bottle contained something other than water, which they shared in the late afternoon. They were typical of the Quechua people in their look—high cheekbones, skin polished by sun and wind in the lofty altitude, feet weathered in sandals made of tires. The bundles wrapped in burlap or woven cloth are seen everywhere.

In line with Quechua fashion, this young woman wears a tall hat and braided hair, with the braids connected in the back. Again, the sadness and weariness in her eyes are evident. Happiness is always relative to expectations. If one's expectations are within one's ability to meet them, happiness results. In my third world travels, I have found that in areas where there is more exposure to tourists the people seem sadder, more aware of their plight. Once exposed to the things of the outside world, their desires and expectations rise and their satisfaction with their own lot in life is diminished. In remote rural areas, people generally seem more content, no matter what the level of "poverty" is in our eyes.

This woman with the captivating smile had approached the stopped train to beg for food. Her joy was unrestrained when she was given a banana by one of the passengers. I love her toothless grin, the wrinkles on her face, her crumpled hat atop her braids, and the layering of her sweaters which defines the seasonality of the photo. I love the motion and energy it exudes; the soft focus somehow adds to the urgency of it.

INNOCENCE FOUND

For every newborn who has ever been *welcomed* into this world, there is sweetness, innocence and peace. This is the beginning of mortal life as it should be. There is nothing spectacular about this picture, and perhaps that is appropriate. We all enter on a level playing field. What happens to us from that point on, however, defines whom we become.

With this photo, the concept for *His Children* was born. During a late-night session in the darkroom, I became very taken by the boy's expression and his outstretched hands. If I hadn't known the answer, I might have wondered "at whom is he looking?" The slight upward tilt of his head and position of his hands imply a question in his mind. What could that question be? It made me think of conversations with God. Perhaps it was the lateness of the hour or the fumes from the photo chemicals I had been breathing for hours. (I prefer to think it was inspiration!) At any rate, I began to envision this photo on the cover of a book. I may even have laughed out loud as I considered who might actually be interested in such a book—other than his parents, grandparents, aunts and uncles. Finally, a more serious thought began to take shape. I finished my work in the darkroom that night. The next day I began to look through the thousands of photos I had taken in my life. It didn't take me long to find what I was looking for—the images that had "spoken to my heart," the ones which left an indelible impression on me. And so, we have come full circle. The rest is history.